ADDING SAFFRON

poems by

William Welch

Finishing Line Press
Georgetown, Kentucky

ADDING SAFFRON

Copyright © 2025 by William Welch
ISBN 979-8-88838-867-9 First Edition
All rights reserved under International and Pan-American Copyright Conventions. No part of this book may be reproduced in any manner whatsoever without written permission from the publisher, except in the case of brief quotations embodied in critical articles and reviews.

Publisher: Leah Huete de Maines
Editor: Christen Kincaid
Cover Art: Colleen Doody, Untitled 2023, Mixed media collage, 30.25" x 20"
Author Photo: Colleen Doody
Cover Design: Elizabeth Maines McCleavy

Order online: www.finishinglinepress.com
also available on amazon.com

Author inquiries and mail orders:
Finishing Line Press
PO Box 1626
Georgetown, Kentucky 40324
USA

Contents

Starch Factory Creek 1
Cain 3
The Pearl of Great Price 4
What Endures 6
Say Goodbye, Catullus, to the Shores of Asia Minor 7
Poem to the Mouse Living in My Attic 9
Hohner Owner 10
Balm/Bomb 11
Nineteen Orchard Street 13
Anamnesis 16
The Flies 18
San Felipe 19
The Exile 20
Horses 22
A Found Photo, Dated 1919, Holland Patent, NY 24
"Steadfast Honey" 25
Familiar Lightning 27
Inheritance 29
Apologia 30
New York Route 29, North of Fairfield 31
Haircut Mantras 33
The New Tenants 35
Ikebana 36
Egg Timer 37
The Border 38
Earth Science 42
Xoc/Shark 44
Vox, Vocis 45

One of Those Guys 47

Freida 49

One Last Season...51

Higby Road at Night 53

The Appearance of Plenty..54

Andrei 56

Dragon Fruit 58

In Praise 60

Chanterelle 61

Dead Horse Bay 62

Toska 66

Icons 67

The Ant 69

Afterlife 71

Criteria for Dreaming 72

Finest Clothes 73

Adding Saffron..75

The Roofers 77

Almost Unmistakably 79

Changes...80

Business Trips to Pittsburgh...82

House Built on Falling Rain 84

"If the world is mysterious, the truthfulness of the image consists in carrying within it a certain mystery as well."
Andrei Tarkovsky[i]

for Colleen

Many thanks to my parents, as well as to Orin Domenico, Ruth Dandrea, and Thomas Townsley for their constant support, encouragement, and help with the writing of these poems. And special thanks to Colleen Doody, whose love and faith in my work made this book possible.

STARCH FACTORY CREEK

> *"Our friends love us and grant us our loneliness."*
> James Wright, "Poems to a Brown Cricket"

On maps it's called Starch Factory Creek,
though people haven't called it by any name
for a long time. If they know the stream,
they may think it's good for fishing in spring.
But they won't catch fish. Waiting, waving a rod
over the water, the line flashing like a vein
underneath the skin of the air, teaches patience—
because in this stream there are no fish.
How long can you stay still?
What do you expect will happen?

The creek grows out of capillaries in mud
and flows downhill southeast of Utica.
Cutting through fields where an orphanage stood,
running in the city's half-derelict park
where we watch it pass us,
its loose brown hair, streaked with white,
tangling around every tree root and stone
fallen in its path, it kneels,
and squeezes like Alice down a narrow archway
into the sewer beneath Bleecker Street.

What are we looking for here?
We decided to go walking, despite the cold,
despite the wind, pushing crows around,
shoving them off the branches of fir trees.
Our own private ritual,
these long walks in bad weather.
The two of us, talking over the cataract of air,
go up and down
crooked staircases built into the creek-carved hills.
Except for us,
the park is empty, eerie in the wind and autumn light.
The fresh snow.

Two old cypresses, standing alone, shudder
like shawl-covered women in a winter scene by Millet.
Exhaustion, a kind of static, pulls them together.
We stop beside the dry lily pond to look at frozen weeds
fastened by ice into brown bouquets,

and you, who know how to see, smile,
leaning over the stalks,
each one a socket of detail you want to memorize.

Meanwhile, I glance around like a tourist
without his camera,
waiting for that—experience.
Part of me is numb, fallen asleep.
Wake up! I want to yell. Wake up!

I watch you. Everywhere,
you seem to find something new.
Your pupil follows you,
trying to observe this or that leaf at your instruction—
the dried remnants of last summer's ferns
curled back into themselves, as if they would bloom again.

We step closer to the creek
and jump, startled
by a single heron
we spooked out of the reeds.
Fighting the wind, trying to fly one way while the air current
forces the bird another,
it struggles through rafters of old trees arched above the water,
wobbles in a gust, flaps harder,
then gives in.
Following the scimitar of wind along its blade,
the heron alights fifty yards away, checked in its mastery.
We hold each other to keep warm, watching
the bird watch us, all three waiting
to see who moves first.

CAIN

It's well-known within our family
I was jealous of my younger brother—
though nothing made me happier
than to make him laugh.
His laughter was like water to me—
water that could clean a wound
no one else knew how to dress.

Are there only seven notes an instrument can play,
sounds we cannot hear? Maybe
there's music that won't fit within a human life—
maybe there are feelings beyond our range.
The keys we play well in are all explored:
love, hatred, friendship, fear, awe, trust, and jealousy.
I have played in each.

We came with our gifts,
my brother with his, simple, too easily prepared,
mine labored over carefully—
why prefer his to mine?

I was never jealous of my brother.
It was someone else—my better self—
who made me feel like a fraud.
And because I could not touch him,
or argue against his accomplishments,
I killed the one who could be killed.

This other man— me-as-I-should-have-been—
he was like a scale with an eighth note.
Instead of fighting him, what if
I let him teach me how to play?

THE PEARL OF GREAT PRICE

for Joel

There were fields around our homes, Joel,
some fallow for a season, others full of maize.
Around them were the woods, in winter
a filigree of witch-fingers clutching at the sky,
in summer, overgrowing every boundary.
Enclosed within the symmetry of corn rows
and houses, we slept well at night, although
boys' thoughts drift and shape-shift.
We could see there was no reconciliation
between the earth and our back and forth
attempts at order. Fences falling groundward
succumbed beneath vines. An orchard grown wild
was our prototype for Eden. Its apples were picked
by deer, or left in the grass as God intended,
rotting with their wasted cider.

In the north country now, I imagine people are burning
leaves. Fire runs through them like a loose dog.
From the hillside, you can see smoke rising, a man
standing there beside the bonfire, watching. A woman
comes out from the house. It's almost a ritual scene.

There are no leaves burning in this yard.
I hear voices from inside the cafe, but I'm alone
beneath a locust tree, drinking coffee,
watching two men in the next yard over
gather tomatoes they grew somehow amid the ruins
of a Brooklyn townhouse. Odd angles, old brick
mold-mottled, and those green, gaunt vines
that twist and zigzag, and branch out, emerald lightning.
The property was abandoned back in March
when they cut the chainlink fence. Together,
they cleared as much of the soil as they could
of stones and glass. Boards protruding from the ground,
like the bones of a half-buried animal, they pulled loose
and set up to hold the twine they used
for a makeshift trellis. They planted their sprouts.

As the season advanced, they appeared more
at home. One of them hung art on the remnants of a wall,
portraits painted by children, his own, I guessed,

faces composed of bright colors that matched
the beans and peppers, and tall sunflowers whose
big dials of yellow petals counted down the hours.

Someone mid-summer tried to mend the fence.
A sign was posted: NO TRESPASSING!
                            PROPERTY FOR SALE.
It didn't stop them. Today, they are laughing,
picking the ripened fruit and vegetables,
gathering the good in baskets, tossing the bad away.
Their joy, their exuberance in their work,
how could it be for just tomatoes?
Whenever I saw them weeding in the sun,
shirts off, sweat curdling through their skin,
they reminded me of the parable about a man
who sold everything he owned in order to buy
the field where he found a hidden pearl.

Have I misunderstood? Maybe that heavy, red fruit
is more than enough. But we lived according to the poem:
living within,
you beget, self-out-of-self,
selfless,
that pearl of great price.[ii]

Joel, we both had to learn that
all it takes to undo a pearl is one cup of vinegar.

WHAT ENDURES

Dusk in Fort Greene Park. I sit watching men
play soccer, weaving among each other
like meadow birds that circle, dive, and hide
among the grass. How do you want to be remembered?
a friend asked me. I had no answer.

On my left, the monument
to soldiers who died aboard prison ships in Wallabout Bay
rises over the treetops. According to one historian,
after the war, our shoreline was covered with skulls
"as thick as pumpkins in an autumn corn field.[iii] "
This crop we sowed, harvested,
is kept here like a seed bank,
the calcium-white, enduring fruit
hidden from view.

How many photographs are there of me?
Thirty-three years of people taking pictures,
my mother, my wife—
someone always has a camera ready.
At work, the manager says
it's time for a photo-op, everyone smile.

The men shout as the ball flies past the goalie—
they throw up their hands,
as if they could grab hold of the sky
and pull it like a victory flag
around their shoulders.

SAY GOODBYE, CATULLUS, TO THE SHORES OF ASIA MINOR[iv]

Peregrinator, passing through small towns,
passing through solitude, what will you remember
about today? Even if you write a few notes

in your book, or record a memo—even if
you assign a room for this quiet place
in that house where you keep memory in order,

your green is not the green of new leaves.
Your recollection of the scent of pine
is imperfect, you discover whenever you break

the boughs of an evergreen. Though somehow when
you recognize that odor, you say—it could be nothing
else. And looking across the river, you see

strange smoke billowing, ragged, dense in spots,
in others a thin discoloration—and call it
without hesitation—green. But you envy the ability

of water to take the shoreline and sky into itself
completely, or only embellished with a few ripples
where midges test the difference between the sky

above and sky below. To go five years without seeing
a face, to go ten—are you sure you can
recognize him? You hope that as with these

details, with odors only occurring in one place,
with colors observed just once a year,
you will know—you will answer,

that is my brother—that is his face—
without thinking, without second-guessing
the glimpse beneath the shroud.

And you will remember—already,
you're preparing yourself—that face
as it was one afternoon

when he pushed you into the current
from the light skiff in which he floated,
beautiful with anger, his arms glistening—

his face like a lily in the middle of a pond,
everything made deeper-seeming by him,
by the weight of his presence. You will remember

his expression once he realized what he had done.

POEM TO THE MOUSE LIVING IN MY ATTIC

I am sick of the dialectic of hunter and prey,
baiting traps with peanut butter while you

find secret passageways inside my cupboards.
What are you doing in my attic now, Lady

Mouse? All day you go unnoticed, but at night,
awake, I lie listening to your back and forth.

The cat hears, too. On patrol, he jumps
off the bed, as I pull the blankets around me,

and imagine what it would be like to live
a slandered life, the way you do.

Vermin, people say. No, master of survival,
you make your nest secure, and because of you

I love more the darkness in my room, the warmth
of my wife pressed against me in her sleep.

I pretend to be your size. Every sense
converts to hearing through the synesthesia of fear.

What is that? Wind plotting against my life,
sharpening its blade of snow.

Four delicate feet, their gentleness unable
to hide their claws. Silence

becomes my house. I know each of its rooms.
I live behind the wainscot of my thoughts.

Still restless, I get up and trace your route
above me, and find cat looking out a window,

as though he heard you crawling, somehow,
through the shingles into an attic above the moon.

HOHNER OWNER

> *a derogatory label used by some blues musicians for people who own Hohner Harmonicas but are unable to play them*

In pictures taken of him during the Second World War,
my grandfather is lean and wears a mustache.
He tears a smile across his face for the camera.

Germany, circa 1944. His unit intercepts a train.
Inside the boxcars, the men find full crates of chocolate,
cameras, and Hohner Echo Harp Harmonicas—

Funny things to ship during war,
I thought as a kid when he told his story.
Could you load G-clefs into your gun,
or kill the enemy with a bent E-flat?
Grandpa was no bluesman.
Bible meeting, that was his style.
He'd rehearse hymns on this harp,
or The Statler Brothers, if he was in the mood.

When I play it now, it warbles like an extinct song bird
brought back to life, trying to recall its key.
I keep it in the original box,
green where the paper isn't worn away,
decorated with Alps and ski chalets.
A man is walking alone toward the mountains.
Germany, idealized. Inside, bright pink paper
lines the box. A tag states:
Hohner Harmonikas sind ein Musterbeispiel deutscher Qualitätsarbeit.^v
As were Panzers. Also the chocolates and camera
grandpa shipped home to his youngest brother (both confiscated in transit).
But he kept the harp.

I wish there were a picture of him when he opened the crate,
expecting rations, or ammunition. Instead, a hundred silver birds
slept in their green cardboard cages.
He took this one and slipped it in his pocket,
a distraction from the earworm whistling of bombs.
And when he played, he didn't care who heard him,
or how his music sounded.

BALM / BOMB

How we went looking for the silent L
when I was a boy! Everyone
who pronounced P A L M
        P Ä M
hesitated as they sang in church,
and tried to add that liquid
to the word B A L M—
for who expects a B O M B in Gilead?
And whose wounds are made whole
with violence?
                      Today is mild,
for October. Even in a t-shirt, it's easy
to stay warm. Sunlight, resinous, unguent pours
honey-thick on evergreens surrounding the garden.
Covers my head, drips over my shoulders and arms.
After a week of cold rain, it does feel like
a balsam-scented oil, soothing my skin…

But I say the word again,
        B Ä M
and wince at the sound of it.
Today's headlines: "President Warns
Russia Against Using Nuclear Weapons"—
"'Dirty bomb' claim in letter delivered to UN."
The skies over my home are clear, although this day,
people like me are enduring *bämbärdm(ə)nt*.
From this garden, I cannot soothe them,
or offer anything other than a half-finished psalm.

Is it better to add in the L,
to curl one's tongue
between the vowel and final consonant,
drawling a little to make the extra sound fit—
or go looking for the other silent one in this pair
of mismatched words, the B burst off the M…?
Or look at dry stalks, all that is left
of summer's bee *bälm*, glow
like copper in this sunlight,
startled by how they look—
burning fuses? Fire
has already touched the explosive.

Is this wrong…? This
yearning for the silent letter? Is it
quintessential?—a belief we hold
because of how the word is written, not how it is spoken?
Only silence marks the difference between
salve used as medicine, and munitions fired in war.
I know from my training
as a nurse—Florence Nightingale honed her skills
in the Scutari Barracks by caring for soldiers.
They died more often of negligence than of bullets,
she learned, and the silent difference
between what is written, and what is practiced.

NINETEEN ORCHARD STREET

> *"He is thinking about something and I know what.*
> *It is not the place he now occupies in my life.*
> *He cannot imagine that, only I can."*
>   Hayden Carruth, "Not Transhistorical Death, or at Least Not Quite"

I am walking through a house that has not changed.
In the basement, there are violets overwintering
under sunlamps, and tomato sprouts, each one a small green fishhook
poking through the soil, barbed with the coming summer.

In the pantry, there are potatoes,
and bags full of yellow onions.
Cans of soup are lined like soldiers on the shelves—
chicken noodle, beef and barley, minestrone.
The old pendulum clock my grandfather winds daily
ticks beside his workshop sink,
one, two, three, four—monotonous
white flower with hours for petals.

Above me, I hear my grandfather's footsteps.
The way he keeps going back and forth makes me wonder
if he is looking for something,
or if he too is counting seconds—
not forward through time, but over and over,
the same seconds, uncertain
of his math, uncertain
if the sum of years balances.

Below him,
I am a root, waiting in the cool darkness.

*

In order to remember today,
I find a place for it in one of these rooms.
My grandfather is the caretaker of my thoughts.
The route to a friend's house he saves for me
in a book of maps in the study.
Some interesting fact about the sun—
that only forty-four percent of its radiation is visible light—
he sets on the lamp stand beside his favorite chair.
To keep the scent of my wife's hair,
I fold a strand of it into blankets in the linen closet,
as if it were a sprig of lavender.

Half-joking, my grandfather warns me,
the moths know what we love,
and where we store old wool inside of cedar chests.

I answer him, Let's save it, then,
within the cupboards of our bones.

*

When he first entered this house as a young man,
he thought time had stopped.
On the kitchen table, a half-eaten meal was set
on dust-covered plates—hardened bread, spotted with mold,
dry, rancid meat. In the center of the table,
a cake sat waiting for someone to light its candles.
One linen napkin was tossed over the back of a chair,
and one was on the floor.

He stood over this grotesque communion
as if the meal had been prepared
for him, for his wife and daughters,
and sat waiting years for their arrival.

But no—something had disrupted the household.
The family that lived here before
left suddenly, and never came home.

On the back porch, my grandfather found half-starved chickens.
Their feathers were ragged.
They had taken out their hunger on each other.
Wounded, bleeding, one of the hens already was dead.

In the bathroom, he found a boy's clothes.
It took months of work, repairing this house.
He and his wife cleared the spoiled food,
they cleaned every room.
Then time jerked forward again.

*

In my imagination,
he stands in the humid July dusk,
looking at the house animated with lights,

watching the shadow play of his daughters in their window,
so I go to stand beside him. Two young men,
the same age, with similar concerns:
how to protect the ones we love,
how to acknowledge our failures,
while taking pride in accomplished work.

And I hear myself asking questions—
If there is light the eyes cannot see,
are there parts of an hour that we cannot count in minutes?

I watch his face, watching to see if and when
he will speak—but he chooses silence.
His voice is kept within him,
like a fragrance.

*

The house is quiet.
I go upstairs, wandering through the living room,
heading for the study where my grandfather spends afternoons
working at his desk. He isn't there.

I stand for a few minutes, listening
to the clock in this room—
there are clocks in every room of this house.
It's an old cuckoo clock he repaired,
one with heavy pine cones dangling from black chains
that drag down the hours toward the floor.
My grandfather pulls them back up every three days.

Through the windows, I see the two big pines
at the far end of the yard.
He's out there, where his gardens used to be—
leveled ground, now, and planted with grass.
I join him under one of the trees.
They are both covered with pine cones,
some brown, newly opened, others still closed, and green.
He reaches up, and tugs on one hanging from the lowest branch,
then his fingers, sticky with sap, search among the needles.
He is looking for a chain.

ANAMNESIS

Ground-thaw at last. We went to dig
holes for trellis posts,
the old man and I, his grandson,
only boy born in a clan of girls.
All morning together,
we turned the auger through brown grass,
a giant key, I thought, twisting in a rusted lock.
I would stop from time to time
in order to catch my breath
and look around the yard, a broad
door closed against us. In my imagination,
I decided we were thieves
digging for a buried treasure—
anything to placate my boredom.
Slowly, as my body warmed,
my mind began to focus on our work, my breathing,
his breath—he breathed hard,
blood flushed his cheeks,
marked with creases, and that one mole
like a button he had grown there to tie his mouth,
and keep him from telling secrets.
He didn't speak much,
though when he thought we had gone deep enough,
that we had picked the lock, he would say
"Pull it up now, pull up."
The soil would tear loose.
We opened the ground and I peered in.
What I saw were stones—like those he had pried
from the dirt years ago, and set into a wall
two feet high between the neighbor's yard and his.
Nothing was hidden here.
No cave.
No secret room beneath the grass
in which people were meeting quietly with maps.
After pulling up a few of these sod corks,
my grandfather broke his silence and said,
"There was an old barn here once.
This must have been a part of its foundation."
That was something new
for my disappointed imagination.
I looked around again,
inventing a farm,
could smell the strong, sour scent of cows,

and rubbed my nose as if I were about to sneeze.
Now, I wanted to dig.
What else was hidden in the mud?
Arrowheads?
Musketballs?
A piece of broken pottery?
At the thought of ceramic, I pictured a woman
holding a bowl of food, reaching it across a table.
Our eyes met, then I followed the line of her neck,
her shoulder, her arm—looked at her wrist,
how the two bones came together
and flowered into her five fingers.
This was her home.
What happened to her?
"We're done digging," my grandfather said.
We had to set the posts in next.
As I worked beside him I suddenly felt
how new I was compared with him.
I looked at his face, tried to memorize it,
tried to memorize the shape of his hands,
arthritic, liver-spotted.
I could smell his sweat as he reached over me.
He was an old man,
working against his age and weakness,
trying to maintain his garden.

THE FLIES

Midsummer. The air is full of flies. Orange, copper,
peach sunshine highlights the stack of books. Everything

is hazy with smoke coming from fires
burning in Montana. Erratic, leaping sideways,

beating against the lip of an empty glass, black clackers
in a fragile bell, the flies throw themselves again

and again. One lands on the table in front of me, wringing
its hands. What a feast it must have eaten, roadkill, a vulture's

leftovers—or it found an open bag of trash. I brush another
fly away from my cheek. And wonder if they are drunk

on my last few drops of wine. Otherwise, what madness
would make them hurl their bodies against the glass,

why would they hurt themselves that way? In the hot dusk,
I soak my feet in a basin full of water. My toes grow pale

as they stay submerged; pain leaves my arches; I paddle
like a two year old in a mud puddle, and tell myself

I should do this more often, I should stop neglecting
what I need. This push toward the farthest extreme—

call it gluttony of the spirit, or call it the vinegar left
when love ages too long in its brown bottles—famishes

the well-fed, and turns thirst into a liquid. There is no more
to drink. The haze is so thick, I can look directly at the sun

while patting each foot dry with a towel. Two thousand miles
that smoke has traveled. The flies have counted every inch.

SAN FELIPE

There is a dry well where water used to be,
where women came at daybreak
with bottles, and clay pots they brought
from Tennessee, gambling this land
would let them live.

A metal grate keeps children safe
from leaning too far over
the open shaft, and falling in.
Nearby, a sign says: This was San Felipe,
the first capital of Texas.
Around the sign is a quiet field
of grass and wildflowers.
A map shows where the meeting hall stood,
where Austin ran a trading post.

The land swallowed whatever people dropped
without complaint, and if I started to dig,
I might find bits of fashioned iron, broken cutlery.
But digging isn't allowed.

Looking down into the well, I fantasize
what it would be like to tie a rope
around one of the oaks
overshadowing the ground,
to climb down this stone periscope into the past.
To find out where the water went.

THE EXILE

Katy, Texas.
In the old train depot this morning,
covered with sweat, I stood reading
graffiti drawn by hobos a hundred years ago.
I can't decipher their patois scrawled across the walls,
but a woman explains that a certain mark meant:
"Stay out."
A warning left for others passing through on the MKT—
they don't like strangers in Katy.

I am a stranger here,
and never can figure out my way around.
I'm used to old village streets in Upstate New York
that follow a canal, or point like a broken compass
at one hill they mistake for north.

Now, in a letter you ask, "when are you coming home?"
That word fills my mouth with the taste of rust,
as though I bit my tongue, and after the shock of it, I think,
what code-word is more difficult than *home*?

In this cul-de-sac, the houses lie
among their trees like packages
sent from someplace far away.
I want to tear them open, see what's inside—
a maquette of family life,
small labels by everyone's feet,
like stage directions in a play?
A bomb?

A few lights come on. The Texas heat abates.
Across the drainage canal, men stop working.
The red earth is piled beside their yellow backhoes
like termite castles. More houses,
more sheetrock and glass, floors leveled, ready for tile.
The prairie holds its breath beneath concrete.
Yellow pine studs rise, a new kind of corn.
I want to run to where the men are standing,
take one of them by the arm, and ask,
who will live in these rooms?

If you were here, you would tell me
I've been reading too many poets obsessed with exile.

One complains of cold on the Black Sea coast,
another writes to friends about spring moonlight
he remembers from years ago, before the wars.
His notes find me instead.
Lorca is marched into a street to die,
and I feel bullet grease on my fingers.
A spear thane, drifting in his boat, says:
the worried ones cannot withstand fate.
A man must hoard his feelings in his chest.
Migraine of the heart—
why feel so far from home?
I am not Naomi:
"the woman was left of her two sons and her husband."
Tonight, I have a safe room with a bed,
a woman is cooking a meal for us in her kitchen.
But there are other women cooking for their children
with rainwater in the garbage dumps of Tijuana.
It's a fact that a boy died this morning of dysentery.
It's a fact that daily two thousand children die from diarrhea.
What they call home I would call,
at best, a shelter.

The poets are selfish, but they try to understand.
They look at fields full of gables and wonder
what animal has been digging in the earth,
and whether or not those still tortoises
will one day move, returning to sea.
They're honest about our chances,
that if we stick our toes in the dirt
our feet will not sprout roots,
and our arms will not grow canopies.
They keep telling us about home
because we keep looking for a new one every day.

HORSES

Alone in the morning fog, Leo's horse is eating grass.
I lean against the railing of a fence and watch.

Last night, he showed me his farm
where rabbits breed to nourish lions
kept at the Syracuse zoo,
and children—his family of eight.
But the boys just left for New York City,
his youngest daughter graduated from high school
back in spring. He lamented—
one son is left in the house, one horse
in the pasture, and one barn full of rodents.

Opening a cage, he pulled out a heavy mass
of fur and ears. "Careful of its teeth."
The shy animal looked at me,
nose twitching, strong legs trying to kick.
I put my hand against its ribs
and felt the rapid throbbing in its chest.
Meanwhile, Leo explained the economics of his business…
Then I turned and saw her standing in the field—
"I always wanted to own a horse," Leo said.
"But I don't know how much longer I can afford it.
I don't really need her."

You're not needed, horse.
It's cold this morning,
and neither of us is needed.

What will happen to us now?
A century ago, if a horse was too old
to work, or injured, men led her
by the nose to Dead Horse Bay,
south of Brooklyn. They cooked her down
and cast her bones in the surf.

But we treat all bodies the same, even our own.
When the last breath is gone from a woman's mouth,
we close her eyes, we tie her ankles and wrists,
and wrap a shroud around her head.
Then the mortician breaks her jaw.

This mare doesn't know her ancestors
dragged Hyksos chariots to war,
or carried Roman merchants.
They fell, thrown from slave ships,
into calm oceans we named for them—
The Horse Latitudes.
I imagine now that I'm standing
beside the rail of a Spanish caravel, looking
up at sails we wet with sea water,
hoping a breeze might drive the ship.
The renewed stillness unnerves me.
What cargo will be next,
since the livestock are gone?

A FOUND PHOTO, DATED 1919, HOLLAND PATENT, NY

for Kim Domenico

A woman sits by a bridge and looks into her own eyes
reflected in the lenses of her glasses,
as if she were talking to her angel,
to her demon—trying to decide—which way
of seeing suits her best.

The river is being led one way,
going where gravity pulls it,
gutting a hillside, making guideways for geese.
The Angel, with her manipulative beauty,
smiles, whispering,
Don't you see the bridge?
You want to leave this town.
Do it.
Follow the road.

But her Demon, cross,
lit from the wrong angle,
shakes her head,
and says, *stay,*
or go where you want,
but make your own road.

"STEADFAST HONEY[viii]"

Fog this morning, after the first cold night in three months.
From my kitchen window, I can hardly see the garden, though

enough light begins to shine through the bank to turn
everything mustard yellow. Outside, my clothes dampen in moments.

The blue cornflowers have withered into gray mop heads,
and California poppies have become their signature small mallets.

Brittle, drying weeds glisten, as though they are made of glass.
Would it be hard to tell the difference between these

and Leopold Blaschka's flowers, each hand-made, blown or lampworked?
No. The has-been wildflowers were not good enough

specimens, dried and pressed, so the glassmaker fashioned his own
blossoms that even after one hundred years never lose their shape and color.

*

While I am here in my yard, safe, though unnerved by the ignited fog,
my friend Lech is six hours into a thirty hour bus ride

between Paris and the Polish-Ukrainian border.
He wrote from his last night to mine, telling me his plans.

For fifteen years, he's had one story in mind, although the text
eluded him. Child of exiles, he is going back to the country

his parents fled. One war then, another today. He will bring his camera,
a few poems he is writing. Unsure of what draws him

to tell this story, equally unsure why he has not been able to tell it,
he is certain now that in the Carpathian Mountains,

there is "a solution waiting to be discovered." That the urge
to make something durable is a kind of homesickness…

*

As the air clears, the garden regains its subtle ranges of color—
faint blue-grays, pinks, greens. One can see the many nuances

of brown. I sit with a guide to botany, testing my memory. There are ways
to identify plants without their blossoms, according to my book…

How do leaves attach onto stems? Are the stems round or squared?
When they do flower, are the blooms symmetrical, or do they fight off symmetry

in favor of imbalance? I doubt myself, and have to check…
to be certain about what I am seeing…yes, that was Indian Blanket,

no, that was Coreopsis, not Black-Eyed Susan. You also can tell by the types
of seed which is which…how poppies, as their pods dry, lift up their tops,

like *nón lá* hats, and little onyx seeds fall into your palm,
a black snow. Blaschka could not capture this with his plants.

*

I close my book, and begin a note Lech will not see for months.
I tell him about the dying flowers, and how I prefer them to glass.

About how I woke last night from sleep—frightened—
of all things—by the thought that I will never understand

the taste of honey. I must bring it to my lips, again and again—
and though some part of the flavor stays steadfast with me,

the whole sweetness is beyond experience. Do bees know better?
I have watched them collect pollen. Each bee thrusts itself

into blossoms the way an excited cat jumps into grocery bags.
One bee goes from flower to flower, and each time before taking flight,

she cleans her face with both fore-hands—as though licking her lips—
full, perhaps, to the point of sickness—but not satisfied.

FAMILIAR LIGHTNING

for William Frankland

Overheated, unable to sleep on this night
of early onset summer, I listen to the neighbor's boy,
up late with friends because it's Saturday.
Their voices, diffused through the humid breeze,
sound closer than they are,
mixed with the smoke-like light of nine o'clock.

"Fire in the hole!" he shouts.
A firecracker pops—innocuous, small explosion.
At the sound of it, my heart beats faster.

Most of the afternoon, he moped, half-asleep
on a swing, typical eleven year old.
I could see him from my kitchen window
while I washed dinner plates, imagining
the feel of grass between my fingers,
instead of porcelain and a sponge.

I remember there is nothing exotic, particularly,
about watching ants, though for a boy
too bored to move, their speed and agility
could become hypnotic…you start to wonder
where it will turn next, how it will climb
up the leg of a dandelion, its black head
peeking over the edge of yellow petals…
But for all the ant's strength
it wouldn't take more than a second—
less—less than a second—with his pinkie—
for him to throw it crushed to the ground.
His boredom keeps him from that, maybe.

But now, he finally has come to life
with matches and knock-off M-80s, laughing
as they blow apart the incomplete darkness,
their momentary blaze, like a camera flash,
almost harmless…

He calls a second time—
who invented those cliché words?
Who taught them to this child?

I close my eyes.
His voice flies away, chasing
the burst echo of his cherry bomb.

Tangled in a sweat-soaked sheet,
I smell the gunpowder.
The boy calls a third time…
Familiar lightning fills the sky.

INHERITANCE

I sit alone holding the September darkness,
cool to the touch, a smooth ceramic,

and think about those who held it the way I do.
My family has eaten meals from this dish, each generation

passed it along the table, a hand-me-down,
like those heirloom spiders, and dust my grandmother swept

off her porch, that came back to find her, the way
birds come back to a tree. These are my inheritance.

If people ask, where do you come from?
I answer, from the spilled flour inside a kitchen cabinet,

from the vines left after their tomatoes are picked.
The autumn sun belongs to me, tucked under the horizon,

like old lace in a cedar chest. I pull it out one strand at a time
to look at the morning, how worn it is, how it still shines.

But I love best this plate of darkness, this September
onto which breadcrumbs have fallen like early snow.

APOLOGIA

> *"And it seems that while others loved,*
> *Strove, hated, despaired,*
> *I have only been busy with listening…"*
>   Czesław Miłosz, "To My Daimonion"

Last summer's foliage still hangs on
the beechnut tree, each desiccated, tawny leaf
a deaf ear. In the falling snow,
there are only two sounds:
a dog barking, and laughter of a crow.

It's possible to go twelve years without talking
with someone, yet recognize their voice
after hearing as few as three words.

But no one teaches us how to listen.
Our parents never sat us down and said,
here, this is like sewing—
to make a finished garment,
you have to pull the thread of my voice
through the fabric of your thoughts.
Often, the needle pricks your thumb.
That is why so many people get upset,
and cut the thread.

I confess.
Like the crow, I enjoy the sound of my own voice.
I'm as repetitive as the dog with his one idea,
and go a long time without hearing you,
the way the beech leaves go all winter
without hearing the wind.

But I am learning. Now,
if I closed my eyes, and you approached
trying to surprise me,
I would recognize you, even by your silence.

NEW YORK ROUTE 29, NORTH OF FAIRFIELD

for my Mother

There are many old barns along these country roads,
piles of gray wood and shingle
slumping, leaning, twisting,
as if a tornado stayed overnight in their haylofts
and nearly knocked them down.
They collapse all of a sudden under the weight
of weathervanes—the old rooster,
caller forth of dawn, caller forth of salvation,
bends over the heap, dropping kernels
of rust onto worn boards.

I think of my mother every time I pass one.
The granddaughter of tenant farmers
who never could afford to buy a piece of land—
cheesemakers, hop-pickers—
she always says, when she sees a ruined barn:
that was someone's dream.

I've made the mistake of thinking she's too nostalgic—
but she's right. This may have been all
her grandparents wanted: this hillside
overlooking the Kuyahoora Valley,
a few fields they could work,
a porch to sit on in the evenings,
as I am sitting on the hood of a car,
watching the late October sunset.
Smoke rises from the house they loved.
A single deer steps through mown grass.
Among a stand of maple trees
lie the remains of a barn they hoped to own.

The idea of buying land is strange to me.
We say, "common as dirt,"
but a handful of dirt costs so much!
My great-grandparents knew.
Rich in apples, richer
in immaterial things, my mother says,
they never held the deed to any home
until their daughter bought a house for them
with money the war department paid out

after her husband died at Anzio.
That's another baffling exchange—cash
for a human life.

The wind picks up once the sun is down,
so I climb back into the car to warm my hands.
Never once has the great-grandson
of the couple who tilled this field milked a cow,
or planted a seed knowing his future
depended on whether or not it grew.
It's been years since I've heard a rooster.

HAIRCUT MANTRAS[x]

for Colleen

If anyone were to ask, what is trust, I can answer
this: letting you pass those scissors beside my ears.

For I have never felt comfortable in a barber's shop,
feeling a stranger's fingers comb through my hair,

or seated on a small white stool, eyes closed, while
my mother tugged at my scalp with coarse brushes.

But our fingers have interlaced, my clumsy ones
with your deft. Now, only you will I let this close.

You ask me to tilt my head, so I do. You step closer,
until I feel your belly press against my back,

and I can count the number of times you breathe
in the minute it takes to trim these few inches.

Cupped in my palms, curled, interspersed with gray
strands, here is three or four months' worth of growth,

still warm. Of all our ways for telling time, this
is the most obvious, individual one. I feel as though

my shadow has been severed with sharp blades.
I feel both relieved and incomplete,

remembering how blond it was when I was a boy…
remembering the soft twist of copper you gave me

when we met, how that ringlet from your head, tied together
with ribbon, was worth more than a wedding band.

But I wonder what about this fiber fixates us—why
must it be styled, or kept under cover? Should I

leave mine long? Mores and stories revolve
around what grows out from human follicles.

While you circle me, I sit reciting my haircut mantras—
"Born of Silence, endowed with strength…

his whole body was shaggy with hair"—
"Washes and razors for foofoos…for me freckles

and a bristling beard"—"for I have been
a Nazarite unto God from my mother's womb:

if I be shaven, then my strength will go from me,
and I shall become weak, and be like any other man."

Cold metal touches the backside of my ear.
I listen to the high-pitched sound as your shears cut.

You tip my chin up with your left hand while
the fingers of your right brush my forehead

clean of trimmings, then travel down my cheek.
And it's clear we understand the risk

makes trust possible, and that trust is like air,
which means this give and take between two people

is a cycle of respiration. Love is the complete breath.
Once finished, you set down the scissors

while I take a broom, sweeping away
that part of myself I no longer need.

THE NEW TENANTS

Senad shook hands, then offered us the keys.
The house his father bought in Utica
after he fled the Bosnian War
was broom-clean, and ready, he said.
We called it ours.
But the man, whose name we don't remember,
left a stump in our yard he used to butcher chickens,
and nearby a pit filled with charcoal and sand.
Rolling the heavy block away from the house,
I saw his fingerprints stained the wood.
My wife found a ring behind a cupboard,
pictures forgotten inside of drawers.
Even roses, mowed flat into the grass,
began to sprout new vines. And I wondered
if he ever imagined us, the new tenants.

That first night, lying awake in the unfamiliar bedroom,
I wondered what it was like for him to sleep here—
adjusting to the rhythm of a foreign city.
At breakfast, we ate our meal by the kitchen window
where he sat with his wife, talking about a home
they never saw again. In the evening,
lounging on the porch waiting
for a new coat of paint to dry indoors,
I watched the August sunlight filter through this silver birch,
Betula pendula. Senad said the old man planted it
because the tree reminded him of Bosnia.

Did he repeat out loud in English *house*,
until the mouth-feel of the word was as familiar as *kuća*?
How could they sound so different, but refer to the same structure?
And why doesn't it bother us more that a house
outlasts its previous inhabitants? Say ours burns—
we feel not loss, but—amputation—
as though the boards and windows
grew around us from our bone and skin.

We plan our renovations.
Within a few days, we've changed the color
in each room, built new drawers for kitchen cabinets.
We like everything. We try to keep the doorknobs clean.

IKEBANA

Out there, you knew you mattered.
People listened. When you spoke,
letters flew halfway around the world.
There were consequences
if you opened the foil backing
of acetaminophen tablets—
this house was paid for, that claim denied.
You enjoyed yourself to a certain extent.
When people at work teased you,
you teased them back, everyone got along.
It didn't matter if they called you Mr. Weathervane,
old rusty rooster. But if so, you were one
who would not turn, even during storms
and kept facing East long past dinnertime.

But here, in this quiet room you love,
where you feel you are almost yourself—
the flowers do not care how you arrange them.
They go on wilting. And to your family,
your rhythmic prayers are just
the mutterings of a drunk father. So few,
so few take on the fiction of their lives.
The flowers arrive fresh every day, but
where are their roots? What force can keep
their petals from dropping to the floor?

EGG TIMER

Because of how hot the forecaster says it will be,
and because the heat takes away my appetite
for anything other than salads, I boil eggs
for tonight's supper early this morning—the time,
exactly 0652 when water starts to roil in the sauce pot.

My windows are fogged, as though an animal
of enormous size stood overnight looking in
the house, its breath steaming up the glass.
Looking through this mist at an overcast sky,
which may produce storms, if only the temperature

would drop one degree, I listen to eggs tapping
against each other, tapping against the pot.
The sound is so close to that of hard-pouring rain
against my roof, and metal flashing around the flue,
that I pretend the storm has come—

and feel comfortably snug, and small, the way I did
as a child on those summer mornings with nothing
to do, just a little practice at listening,
while the slow simmer of distant thunder heightened
the stillness. Here I am, enjoying my delusion,

enjoying, even, the mild discomfort of being
a little too warm—so it's hard to imagine now,
at 0657, with five minutes more to wait,
that people are dying in Yemen, in Gaza, and Ukraine—
that come Sunday, it will have been two months

since nineteen children were murdered. These lives
ended in less time than it takes to cook an egg.
What can I do? How small a kettle rage is.
It's 0702, and no rain. I drain and rinse the eggs
in cold water, then open the porch door.

Outside, the air is over-laden with moisture. Everything
is dripping wet. In a pot, four young milkweed plants
show signs that monarch caterpillars have hatched.
I bend a leaf upward carefully and see one,
a small life, like ours, with an uncertain future.

THE BORDER

Each morning, I wake in the dark
and move quietly through this house
without turning on any lights.

In the bathroom, at last
I flip the switch. One hand condenses
out of shadows—another hand
leans on the countertop—
two feet are standing on cold tile.
Across the mirror, that fence of glass,
I see my face.

It's the confusion of being
in this frontier between sleep
and wakefulness that makes me
look a long time, unsure
of where I am.
I have to understand, again,
this face is mine,

and try to enter the territory of my senses.
I look at my arms,
my chest expanding with breath, ribs flexing—
surprised by how whole I seem.

But who are these people who think
they possess an identity?
They tell others, no, this is mine,
you are not welcome,
I will not share.

I possess nothing, not even this body.
I wander in its peculiar wilderness,
learning my way around.

*

Cold water on my skin, in my mouth.
Fully awake, I tell myself
I've been dreaming—

Routines propel me.
I go to work where I become
a cartographer, feeling for rivers
in a person's wrists, counting
mountains in their eyes.

And who am I now?
A collection of tasks,
the name written on a wall,
the set of scrubs hovering over a sick-bed.

A stroke robbed this old woman
of her voice—
she can only nod yes or no. But she listens
when I speak, looks up.
Here again, that border—
a human face—
a pair of eyes, a brow, nose, and chin,
her mouth, hungry for water and words.

I rest her head, pale, fragile
on a pillow.
One word keeps us separate.
You—means: other.
Without that word, I might think
I was my own nurse,
I am the one who cannot breathe.

*

City of refugees, Utica,
I drive home on its syncopating streets.
I pass yards where families are grilling lamb—
fast-food dives are full—
restaurants, kitchens flavor whole neighborhoods
with their scents of grease and garlic.
The smell of cooking food
is to the city what sweat is to the body—
one's odor, sour, sweet, salty, simultaneously
repellent and attractive.

There are people who love this town,
they were born in its hospitals,
or came here from war-ruined countries
looking for a quiet place to live, safe—
but for many of us, this America,
a rubble of factories, long hallways of maples,
vacillates between the common and uncanny.
For many of us, it is not safe.
I know this place well, and because I know it well,
I am easily lost.
Everything looks strange,
the way only the familiar can.

*

In the dusk, my neighbors are sitting on their patio.
An older couple, they want things clean.
Their yard is neat, their lawn mowed exactly.
Few ornaments clutter the house,
only tomato vines and a single rosebush.

The husband speaks little English,
but we talk in other ways.
Side by side in March, we cut back the hedges
between our properties, raked leaves.
We drank German beer, standing together,
a reversal of each other,
my body his thirty years ago,
his the body I will have.

His wife calls me, and I wave.
She is a kind woman.
And she is proud, of this yard, of her house.
It isn't vanity, it's a form of joy,
like waking early in winter,
bathing in hot water,
and looking through the steam at your legs.
You smile—and say, those are part of me,
and I am glad.

*

Everything settles into the new darkness,
breaking up, like bread in a bowl of water.
This heavy body is filling up with sleep,
the way a marsh fills with rain,
and I trek through the low-country
of my feeling, those places where
life and death are indistinguishable.

One more time, I stand on my side
of the barricade, and look across at you.
Why are we caught like this, close together,
but separated by such a skin?
Make an incision. One little cut.
It might be enough for you to crawl through.
I do not want to stand here
on this side of the fence alone.
Come join me.

EARTH SCIENCE

I miss that rock shop in Katy, Texas
where my younger brother took me one Tuesday,

and where I stayed for three hours,
studying the facets of flashy amethysts.

He showed me opals that glowed
beneath black lights as green as frogs,

and big slabs of petrified wood, remnants
of ancient palm trees whose bark I touched,

whose rings I counted, wondering in what year
according to human calendars each grew.

The more I looked at fossils and sediments,
ultramarine lapis flawed with pyrite,

mineral splotches on granite, as irregular as
liver spots on an old woman's hands,

the more I realized I love imperfections,
the intricacy of nuance—and here I claimed rocks

were boring when I was in high school.
Along with the other boys, I made fun of our earth

science teacher, who wore a comb-over
and had hairy arms and knuckles. We laughed if he said

cleavage. But when it was my turn to put drops
of acid on limestone, and watch how rock fizzed,

melting away like snow, the change enthralled
me. I couldn't explain. Maybe I didn't want to

admit what was happening. By then, I too had
hair on my arms as thick as Esau's. I was jealous,

afraid the other boys would taunt me
and my curiosity. For whose love was I competing?

Whose blessing did I want back then, so badly
I couldn't embrace my difference? Was it theirs?

Why did I laugh at what I thought was so serious?
Now, I am the one who has the power to bless.

My house is filled with stones from all over
the continent—fragile shales found

in Starch Factory Creek that shatter as easily
as old glass; New Mexican turquoise; brown

granites brought down from Adirondack peaks;
enough marble to start my own museum.

I know that once they are relieved of the pressure
that made them, diamonds will thaw back into graphite.

XOC / SHARK[xi]

Synecdoche—
to think of sharks, I think of their teeth,
one tooth, the letter V held in my palm…
So, when I learned that some believe
the English word "shark"
comes from the Mayan word "xoc,"
and "xoc" can also mean "count," I smiled.
Of course! One counts all of those teeth,
an endless-seeming wave of bone, up to fifty-thousand
produced over the course of one shark's life.
Too bad there's an instance of the word "shark"
in an English manuscript from the fifteenth century,
before anyone in Europe used the word "Maya,"
or thought to write "xoc" with a "x,"
that letter which, in English, we pronounce "z,"
as in "xenophobic Anglo-Americans
didn't believe the Mayans were civilized,
despite all those pyramids and calendars,
and thus could not have a writing system…"
But for the Mayans, the "x" represents "sh,"
so "X-O-C" is pronounced "SHAHK,"
as in what the "shark" does when it smiles at you
and all you can do is "count" the seconds left before it bites.
Where does our "shark" swim from?
Xocingly, from the German word "Schurke,"
which means "scoundrel," but also gave English
"shirk." Shark. Shock. This is self-indulgent play,
yes, so I will return to *sə ˈnekdəkē*—
To think of people, I think of our mouths,
our lips parting, opening, joining, pursing,
smiling, frowning, forming a kiss
and plosives—our finite teeth, all fifty-two,
easily knocked out, irreplaceable—
and our tongues behind them,
like caged birds which struggle to fly,
but cannot, and so flutter against out teeth
and lips, forming vowels and affricates.
This is what I think about when I want to think about us:
how our mouths say, "xoc," and "shark,"
these nests for the birds we call "language" in English,
and in Mayan, "T'aan."

VOX, VOCIS

The air hoards voices—and so many
sounds: distant sirens, the neighbor's children
chattering along with starlings and chickadees.
Old men outside bodegas, gawking, gossiping.
Underneath these, the paper-like crumpling
of dry leaves, as though the air was writing
everything down, compulsively taking notes—
*what did he say? Something about voices,
something about birds.*

The air ought to ripple when we speak
the way a pond does when it rains.
Water becomes saw-toothed, jagged,
just so the air is sharpened by a human voice.

To think, there are deserts of silence—
like the moon, that fish hook dangling from a tree.
There, in craters that never once ricocheted echoes
off their stones, we would die. We couldn't bear it.
There can be no more inhuman place.
Imagine yourself without a voice,
unable to say one word, unable to lean over
to someone you love and whisper in her ear.

Not here. Here, we are always talking—
almost too much—until the sky seems like a jar
of voices knocked over on the floor.
I'm on my hands and knees, trying to sort them,
trying to trace one back to you.

But why this noise?
Why do we feel incomplete until someone hears us?
Because part of each of us remains children,
and cannot live if we go unnoticed?
That is our first act: the cry,
the only thing we can do
to call the ones who know us:
come from the other room!
Then who are we crying out for when we sing?

Here I am—this voice
is mine, no one else can use it.
Yours sounds sure, confident.

Our conversation continues—
our only fear the thought we might be stifled
and our voices left wilting
like cut flowers in the vase of our mouths.

ONE OF THOSE GUYS

in memory of Gerald Stern

You've known one of those guys,
haven't you? The one who brings the heavy
subjects into every conversation?
He always starts with a casual remark,
if odd, like how he sometimes compares
himself to a moth—not really
in the spirit-animal way—and not
an adult moth so much as a caterpillar.
You think, oh, ha ha, a self-deprecating
joke, I got you bro, but before you can
smooth out the grin, he's broached
all the "issues," from the problem of love,
to the blunders of Congress, and
has even made references to
Talmudic exegesis, all without taking
a breath, all while holding a cup of coffee
the barista overfilled—and you can't help
wondering how on earth he's going
to get that all the way to his mouth
without spilling it. What's even more
impressive is the steadiness
of his hands, because he will hold
that overfull cup still for half an hour
while he steers your discussion from
Shakespeare's identity to neoliberal capitalism
and how we've all been convinced
to turn our lives into commercial products…
It's a delicate task, for sure, weaving
this conversation in and out of the road
blocks of small talk and conventional opinion.
Maybe he secretly believes he's a nuisance,
that people take him for a nutty
Cassandra, running around town weeping.
But I wouldn't say that. Because he is funny,
and warm—someone I'm always
glad to see, although afterwards I'm a little sore,
as though I'd been lifting crates of books,
or holding a two-by in place, waiting
for my partner to drive a screw into the wood.
It's a kind of pain you feel all over
and take some amount of pride in because

you can say you got something done…
Just the other day, I was telling a friend
of mine about how my wife and I
raised monarchs this summer, from egg
to full-blown butterfly in four weeks—
we had nineteen, in total—and don't you know,
this guy had the nerve to ask me if
I was going to be sad when they went extinct?

FREIDA

for my Father

On my way home after
working nightshift at the hospital,
I see wreckage common here in Utica
at winter's end—two deer carcasses
tossed onto snowbanks beside the road.
Of course, I think about their fawns, old enough
to be on their own—oblivious.
And I think of human children—
times when I have seen
one in a park, crying alone.

Because no death is insignificant,
because I'm too tired to mourn
these bodies lying there
like a pair of dolls forgotten outside after playtime,
I speed up. Concentrate on the stoplight,
and how the March sky graduates from indigo
in the west, to light blue, to pink.

I have no idea where they go—the struck animals: deer, raccoons…
Someone has that job. Later this morning,
he will load their bodies onto a truck and drive off…
Our bodies, left over, excess
once our breath goes out of us,
are wheeled into the hospital basement on gurneys.

Somewhere in this Upstate county
my great-grandmother is buried—
dead at twenty-seven after her husband abandoned her
and their young boy, my grandfather.
I can't remember her name—maybe Freida.
Maybe she had brown hair, like me, and blue eyes, like her son.
Maybe like her great-granddaughter, my sister,
she preferred darkness,
preferred the mystery of life and death
over our numerous and unsatisfying mythologies.
I have gone looking for her all over the countryside,
wondering how much of the earth's
calcium comes from human bone,
and have spent I don't know
how many hours trying to read the names

engraved in worn marble, running my fingers
over the surface, like a rock climber reaching
for a hold on a sheer outcropping, no pitons
to drive into the past, no ropes…

I wish I knew how her hands felt
when they closed around her child's,
and whether she had dimples, or crooked teeth.
I keep asking her silly questions in my mind—
what is your favorite flavor,
did you enjoy math or English?

We used to believe that
if we did not honor the memory
of our mothers and fathers
they would set up obstacles for us.
If our negligence went on long enough,
they would come to find us in our homes, demanding
glasses of wine, meals
cooked for them as they cooked
for us. Our ancestors, we thought,
do not lose their thirst or hunger.
They do not stop loving
the sound of human voices.

ONE LAST SEASON

That is a red maple and even a young child would know
it is dying. The central leader is already deadwood—

bark sloughs off whenever storms come—every week
or so I clear my yard of sticks and branches, some

long wands, stout once, now soft with rot, some
twigs a bird might use for nest weaving, if only

they wouldn't fall apart as you pick them up. But,
half of the crown is still alive, still each autumn

the tree turns that Holy Spirit crimson, like Jesus
touched the trunk on his way to Emmaus—

so, despite how close the tree is to my house,
and how I keep saying each fall, "this is it,

one last season," come February, when winter
buds start to swell, and one good thaw makes spring

and all that rebirth seem more than poetic trope,
an actual resurrection, the tree remains standing

there by the foot of my driveway, minus a few limbs,
yes, looking gaunt and thin, like James Baldwin

in June, 1987, when the cancer was already too deep,
eating through his stomach, though he persevered

daily, sat in front of a stack of paper
that had its own life once, before it was pulped—

and who could cut down a tree that calls to mind
a man like him? Well, sad fact, my neighbors

to the right and left would like to see Art's
Tree and Stump Service show up with chainsaws,

whether or not the tree reminded them of Jimmy,
or John the Baptist, because "it's a liability, you know."

I'm out in my yard again, picking up more bark—
long, spongy sheets of it that feel between my fingers

like little more than wet mulch, and I look up
at the gray limb it peeled off from overnight

during a heavy rain. I imagine a dying man,
no longer strong enough to swallow small sips

of water, whose fingers have grown cold, but
whose thready pulses in his wrists press blood

forward to his thumb, which runs back and forth
along my thumb. We're all going to go to pieces—

we're all going to sit at the table with four ounces
of red wine in front of us and wish the taste were enough

compensation for the crushed fruit. I see another strip
of bark caught on some branches that are quick still,

each shaking a fist of red buds, like a man about to
roll dice. Mercy, as Baldwin might suggest,

is what's called for now, and more than mercy,
love, which comes at an unbearable price.

HIGBY ROAD AT NIGHT

It's easy to get distracted on old roads like this,
that zigzag up and down wooded hillsides,
as if deer laid them out,
and hunters following stomped them into place.
Dangerous, clear nights—
in the valley below, the lights of Utica shine like sparks off a weld.
Above the hill, the full moon is rising.
In town, it looks no brighter than a doctor's penlight,
shining down chimneys, but here, I understand
our impulse toward praise that transfixes us.

In time, I see the road swerve.
It drops in a syncope toward the river.

A girl I knew died at this curve. Nineteen years old.
It was 3 a.m., she was driving home from her boyfriend's house
and somehow, because she was tired, almost asleep,
she missed the turn.

I remember her mother—pregnant with her.
She used to cut my hair when I was a boy.
In the mirror, I could watch her face, and saw her belly
bulging her smock forward as she circled my head,
running her fingers through my hair.
I didn't understand what it meant, that girth—
or how the body worked.
Birth was as mysterious, and as unlikely, as death.

When her daughter died, I didn't know what to do. I drove
over the route, looking at the trees,
following the yellow and white nerves of the road,
wondering how they failed her.

Old, battered rock, the moon
was there that night. Maybe
it was the moon's fault.
It didn't scream, or hold its breath.
It didn't cry, or bother to warn her.
All it could do was smile,
as though that would be enough,
as though it thought
the phases of human life are like its own—
birth, growth, waning—
only a night or two would go by without her.

THE APPEARANCE OF PLENTY

Two weeks after Christmas. It is cold in T.J.'s Market—
no lights inside, other than that pale blue light filling windows,

which look like small banners of winter sky, the drab,
gray flags of a forgotten country. Many of the wooden

stands are empty, save for gourds leftover from the holidays,
and several dozen apples, each apple spaced apart

to ape the appearance of plenty. Cardboard boxes are heaped
against the walls. In one, there are red stains

where crushed fruit soaked the paper, then dried, leaving
a kind of wavy scar. They contain only the vague,

sour musk of raspberries. Odors of peach. Citrus. Everything
is overripe, everything smells of wet earth and roots.

The greenhouse, still cluttered with wreaths, where each spring
my mother bought marigolds and begonias, where

I smelled basil for the first time, is where I find
T.J. standing alone, like a single fruit tree planted in a glade

of cut and pruned evergreen. "Anything I can help you with?"
he asks, and I answer, "Just looking." I should have known

not to come here—that this has become one of those stores
where you never find what you need, and never leave

without making some purchase. But where should I have gone
instead? What orchard or supermarket around here sells

the silver apples of the moon, the golden apples of the sun?[xii]
I check the varieties T.J. has for sale, typical Macintoshes,

Empires, Galas; the flavorless Red Delicious; the Granny Smith,
and Pink Lady. They are already soft, cider-pungent.

I handle them afraid to break their skins. All the same, some
might cook well with cinnamon and butter in a pie.

I pick three—no—five—and carry them to the counter
to wait for T.J. who is back there in his temporary forest

pulling up his roots from a concrete floor, sticky with sap,
who is coming forward now, smiling

dryad, loosening his bark, opening his blossoms.
"How's your mother?" he asks, and I look at him, startled

he recognizes me. It's been fifteen years, at least, since
I saw him. "She's good," I say, trying to guess what news

spread around, whether I will have to explain. He punches
at the register with his finger. I recount the apples,

wondering if they are the ones I saw once fall from their tree
during a thunderstorm, hard, clenched fists pounding the earth.

ANDREI

The table where you sat waiting for me, Andrei,
was wet with rain, little blisters of sky.
You had tea ready for both of us.
A bee hovered around your ear
and you leaned away from it, as a child might
lean away from his mother's kiss.

How did you find my house?
Surprised to see you, I wasn't sure
of what to say, and stood on my porch steps.
Your dog wagged his tail beside my legs.

You look like your photographs, of course,
and I'm disappointed that you answer
my first question—
how does a man look in the afterlife?—
with the familiarity of your face.

But you aren't incongruous here,
and that's why I am so confused.
If my neighbor saw us,
he might think you were my father.
Is that how ghosts stay incognito?
To others they are just strangers—
only those they haunt know who they are.

Why of all ghosts have you come?
I wasn't thinking of you when I woke.
There are many people I love
but haven't seen in years.
I've sat here waiting for them—
but you have undone my locks,
boiled water as if you were at home,
set out plates and knives.

Toast with butter, a few plums,
their rose-tinged juice dripping
onto your napkin—
you eat your light breakfast.
Finally, I sit down.
Does the burden of explanation rest with me?
I will try: this is an accident.
On my way home from buying coffee

I turned down the wrong street.
We're raised to think the otherworlds are invisible;
there's a distinction
between inner and outer,
life and death—
but you can see Dante's Heaven
if you wait for night,
and the doorway to the land of the dead,
according to poets, is a lake in Italy.
Are you here to forgive me?

You offer me a cup with a candle in it.
That little flame
reflected in the orange-brown tea
makes a small cross—
and this has been my problem all along:
how to quench my thirst
without burning my lips.

DRAGON FRUIT

It was one of those things you think you'll never be able to find again
and hold for longer than it takes—to guess the weight—set down, pick up,

put back—finally carry with you. Dragon fruit. You have to taste it some time,
I told myself days later, choosing an apple for lunch again.

Stood over the sink, cutting it apart, thinking of what it was—pink and white
petals—a rose-shaped bloom—even thought I could hear the apple

buzzing, as though the bee that pollinated it was still trapped inside,
dying of sweetness. While I ate, I sat reading about pitayas,

looking at pictures of *Selenicereus*—a cactus, or, rather, a bouquet
of living snakes, tied together by their tail rattles—and this—the moon flower.

It flares open at night, cobra-hooded, an open mouth full of pale yellow
fangs. Imagine stumbling on it in the dark—imagine

if such a thing acted the way it looks, if it were to bite your wrist…
What flavor could this fruit have, which grows from a blossom

born at sundown, dying the following morning—an intense life,
lived between dusk and dusk? I heard it reminds people of strawberries,

but I doubted that. It must taste like death by flower.
Anyone who eats of it will know it was not meant for us.

*

The many ways of distracting oneself eventually fail. I finished
my last piece of apple. Restless, unsure of what to do,

I went outside. Two weeks since a hard frost.
There was work to do around the house. So I got my rake and gloves,

tried to keep myself busy. Concentrated on the motion of my arms,
listening to the drag of dried leaves across the flowerbeds, the sound

ssshhh, ssshhh, ssshhh, soothing. I looked for signs the milkweed
my wife planted in July made it through winter. Our monarch rescue plan.

They need this plant to survive, as do others—a type of red beetle,
with black spots and curving antennae, like longhorn cattle—ambush bugs,

that wait inside of flowers, their forearms as swollen as a body-builder's…
Warmed, sweating a little, though the air was cool, I stopped

long enough to look the bed once-over. Too long, because I saw lying
in among the dried, snapped-over stalks of evening primrose

the woman, unconscious on a gurney—could feel the snapping of her ribs,
the announcement overhead—*Code Blue*. I went back to work, telling myself

don't think about it—focused on the rake's tines, how they de-thatched
the grass, bending back under pressure, like someone's knuckles

so the look of them hurt…*Please keep going*
her daughter cried, begging us. Watching.

Fifteen minutes. Twenty. Thirty, finally
the doctor took her aside. Finally,

I let the rake drop and stood weeping, alone in my garden, holding
my grief in my palms, as though it was a kind of fruit I had never seen before.

*

After several days, the deep red of the pitaya began turning pale.
A small brown spot had formed. For something that sprouts from plants

that resemble serpents, the dragon fruit itself looked like a species of parrot—
or rather a comet that survived its fall earthward, still on fire,

exuding little wings of green smoke. It perched in my hand, and I wondered,
how should this be eaten? Peeled, pared, and served cold?

Is it better cooked? Can I just put it to my lips? A knife passed through
without resistance; halved, the inside reminded me of spiders'

egg pouches—that kind of almost-white, the swirling fibers—tying knots
around small seeds. What scent it had was floral, like fresh tulips.

And the flavor—I scooped out the fruit with a spoon, big chunks, trying
each while thinking, how can this be? I ate one piece after another,

with each, asking myself, where is the sweetness? Where is the venom?

IN PRAISE

> (lines in quotes are from Robert Bly's poems "The Pistachio Nut," "Listening to Old Music," and "Hiding in a Drop of Water")

> for Orin Domenico

"Like a note of music, you are about to become nothing."
Is that what the trumpet tells the trumpeter?

He puts his lips to the mouthpiece, and sees a face
reflected in the brass with an ant eater's grin. He breathes

in, as though he is about to blow on the first coals of a cold
fire, then gives all of his breath to E flat. Next what?

It's funny the way snow seems permanent in late January.
Small flakes keep falling, trees bow under the weight.

Maybe it isn't mass that makes gravity work.
"Maybe silence. The speed of the soul leaping over fences"

while the shoveler goes on spading snow creates that
sense of falling toward a center. When it's quiet,

I feel how heavy my bones are. I want to sing,
even if what I sing has no melody, just a low hum,

a groan, like the Bedouin women used to mourn.
"Well, music, go on growling about God."

I like the way an alto saxophone comes apart
at the end of the night—how the reed pops out

like the tongue of Orpheus when the Maenads butchered him
because he spent too much time alone singing.

The drum kit and the trombone both try to warn us—
"Whatever happens to me will also happen to you."

This snow is already melting. If you look close, you can see
the names of all the rivers of the world.

I stop a moment to watch my breath rise upward—
"I am ready to praise all the great musicians."

CHANTERELLE

It's singing weather.
As the wind gains strength, I watch
from the safety of my home
those three big spruces bend,
their grackle-black branches wrenched
like a child's arm,
and know how small I am—some mushroom
beside Rabelaisian giants, an ant
covering himself with mountains of sand.
I peek out my oculus, then duck,
humming
an upbeat tune my grandfather liked,
or chanting,
my voice half shout, half whimper,
one of those hymns
my mother taught me…

That is some comfort,
growling at storms, facing the inevitable
with music. A howl
from outdoors induces
a caesura—
counting the rest, I turn to an open book which says the word
"chanterelle" refers to that one string
on lutes and ouds
strung alone, not paired in courses.
When the luthier tuned his instrument,
he tuned it according to that string.

The text indicates also
that through some hiccup in language,
chanterelle means a type of "edible woodland mushroom
with a yellow funnel-shaped cap and a faint smell
of apricots…" They look like small ears
listening on the forest floor.
Maybe they can hear the high note
according to which this earth is tuned,

and if so, should I match my voice to their pitch—or the wind's?
Or whose human voice?
Who now hears the C an octave above praise,
and knows we are together, a choir
trying to harmonize
in a broken egg?

DEAD HORSE BAY[xiii]

Do not walk barefoot here.
The sand is strewn with glass.
Ruinous and inchoate at once, the shoreline recedes
toward Rockaway. March. Wind
spits rain at the ocean's face.
Gulls hover in a landward breeze. At the edge of the beach,
above the tide's limit, seven-foot tall reeds form a cane-break,
dry, brittle, soughing. I have entered
a flowerbed of bones.

A hundred years ago, Manhattan sent its chattel here,
old animals, no longer capable of work,
the wounded, the obstinate.
Butchers slaughtered horses
by the thousands. They dumped offal
into the bay, but tide by tide the sea returned their offering.
Crouching, I find white blossoms
growing out of the sand—ribs, pasterns, pieces of a horse's knee.
This cemetery the butchers made
has become a garden.

Nearby, moss-carpeted boards form floors, a driftwood house
without walls, without a roof.
Careful of where I step, feeling
one moment I'm intruding, the next, proprietary,
I walk from room to room.

When the rendering plants closed, the city used this place
as a landfill—as though we expected the sea
to remember our lives for us,
to clean away our history.
Both what we loved and what we disowned,
what we brought to life, and what we tried to drown.
Just as the sea returned the horses,
it returns our garbage. Half-buried
dinner plates, shattered, shine through the sand.
Cough syrup bottles, old jars
filled with pebbles roll forward in a wave,
roll back. Water dabs its salve
across the cheeks of a ceramic doll, its skull lying broken
beside oyster shells. The ribs of a derelict
yacht lie keel-over in a dune,
as if the makeshift sea were a junk dealer

fashioning a model for a modern whale.
And shoes. Hundreds, some reduced to their soles,
others intact, even with laces, step forward
from the surf, as if a whole city
of men and women, like myself,
were stepping out of the calm waves,
followed by a shadow of birds.

*

Distant enough from Brooklyn,
there are only three sounds here—
the sound of rain pelting sand,
the sound of wind in dry grass,
the sound of water washing over glass.
Small waves, delicate, curled,
like a boy's fingers arched
over piano keys, chime
glass against glass. Accidental music.

I remember this.
I remember sitting at the keyboard on summer afternoons, the song book
closed, pressing keys down
so gently, the hammers only made the strings tremor rather than resound.
What my hands played,
I heard, unsure if the music was in the piano,
or in me, or if it traveled through an open window
missing half its notes—a song
someone else was rehearsing in another house.
I listened, trying to recognize a melody,
until I crossed the point at which the hammers touched the strings
without making a sound.

That was not music
I could play again, or play just once.
It was not a text notated,
bearing time signature, and key.
I could not reproduce it then,
but recognize it now. Intuition insists
this is what I heard. Knowledge is reproducible, intuition
is not. Knowledge depends on time,
intuition recognizes time to be
a house with many rooms, whose windows overlook separate streets…

We look through, we say time has a single outcome,
but intuition implies time
takes every direction, not only one. Look again,
choose a different window…

*

The water moves back,
pauses,
rushes forward—
a respiration. Each breath brings out another note.

I walk close to the cane-break, listening.
Wind moves through the reeds,
bending, snapping them.
There is no sign yet of any regaining green.

All around are traces of what this place was,
or what it will be. It is confusing
to stand here, to wonder if those are my shoes
washed up by storm surge,
if I am one of the butchers walking home after work, a man
who smells iron everywhere, the stench of rotting meat.
I think about my life, how it may be
a perversion of sacrifice—
the sea, god of horses, received their blood,
not as tribute, but out of convenience.
I picture the water blossoming, becoming a greenhouse of poinsettias,
imagine the rocks clotted, the waves frothy with albumin…
I think about how we abuse our own bodies,
lead people into the killing room.
What escape is there? Where would I go if I could get away?

Closer to the surf, the sand is covered with thick mats of seaweed,
kelps, and thin grasses. A few tires,
and rubber skirts from traffic drums lie scattered around.
What if I walk down to the water?
If I follow the horses in?
What kind of return
would the tide bring about?

It takes faith
to put corn and squash into the ground,

to hope the seeds grow. What faith
those men laboring in the slaughterhouse had,
to plant bones in the sea!
One day, the crop of new horses will come,
the whinny of a wave announcing them.

I kneel, a gardener among his calcium roses.
I pick one white flower,
a blossom to carry with me,
a boutonnière.

TOSKA[xiv]

I've been waiting, thinking of you
without words, feeling your absence
in my body, like a sprain,
and hold still to keep from hurting.

Page after page, I searched anatomy books,
trying to localize the pain, and found
diagrams of organs that showed
how they filter blood,
where ligaments attach
muscles to bone—nothing corresponds
with this injury.

Gradually, I came to learn
how many ways of waiting there are.
Each has its unique problem.
How many times had I thought,
we missed our chance?
You opened the wrong door.
I was in the wrong room.

There is a kind of patience that knows
how to pull water out of stones.

Voices, shadows on the street—
none are yours.
Porch doors slam hollowness through houses.
My eyes carry this message to you
block by block like dromedaries
under a green sky.

ICONS

> *"We need better images."*
> Werner Herzog in *Werner Herzog Eats His Shoe*, by Les Blank

> *"If the world is mysterious, the truthfulness of the image consists in carrying within it a certain mystery as well."*
> Andrei Tarkovsky

Across from the bus stop at Myrtle and Franklin Aves,
a barbershop is framed by brick houses, one yellow,
one sun-faded red, both stained with rust.
On the shop roof, off-set to keep the composition askew,
a white chimney points like an apostle's finger
toward sheet metal balconies where shirts dangle from the railings
in place of prayer flags. Wind works them, wringing
grace and wash-water on whomever waits below.
Black wires craze the sky. From their nest in the shop's eave,
starlings poke out their heads, like people peeping out of windows
in an icon of Christ walking the Via Dolorosa.
See how he suffers? I ask the birds, but they are too busy
to notice, sitting on their little circle of eggs.

*

We're all aware of each other's eyes
on the city bus. Each face renders its character well.
Rublevs, Goyas, Freuds, a Titian-esque Diane.
Bacon's Screaming Pope is seated at the wheel.

How to capture the spirit in a glance,
isn't that the portrait maker's dilemma?
Suggest bones
beneath the skin, show the tell-tale skull.
At the same time, recover an expression
of the child.

The bus stops for a red light and I look out the window.
A young girl is standing with her back pressed against the wall
of a bodega, both hands splayed over the bricks.
Next to her, two men lean into the April sunshine drinking sodas.
She peeks around the corner then pulls back,
tensing, smiling. Curious, I sit forward and see
a toddler in a baseball cap waddling beside a fawn colored pug.
Then the bus pulls me away…

*

The botanic garden is crowded this spring morning.
It's hard to move around. People float along the paths
as though their feet have been erased.
The gravel covering the ground is all that's left
of those marks that were their legs.

A flâneur, I circle the Japanese pond.
Someone hidden behind a stand of yews
is reciting an old poem:

>   *The thought frightens us*
> *That this planet with all its darkening geese*
> *Was created not for union but for separation*[xv] .

What do you think of that? I ask my shadow.
Where a poplar overhangs the path,
my shadow crouches beside the water.
We look together at one branch,
half-submerged, leaves and all, in the pond.
The leaves move slowly with a current,
and catch the sunlight, shimmering,
a sunken treasure. Without a splash,
my shadow slides in,

and I, alone now, watch
red-eared sliders swim like dislocated islands
through the pond. One who went ahead of them bathes
its out-stretched neck in the sun, clutching a rock.

A trail of ants leads uphill to a Shinto shrine.
There, the statue of a fox sits, waiting.
Its sculptor followed the wood-grain to shape the fur.
The ears are rain-worn. Ants have chewed into its paws.
Spirit, I say, teach me the right prayers.
Where I come from gods are indifferent,
and I don't know the words.

THE ANT

> *"To humankind, these Others are purveyors of secrets, carriers of intelligence that we ourselves often need… We receive from [these creatures] gifts…Yet they remain. Other to us, inhabiting their own cultures and displaying their own rituals, never wholly fathomable."*
> David Abram, *The Spell of the Sensuous* p. 14

The ant, rearing on hind legs, continues its search
along the glass rim, turned over on my countertop.

"That's a carpenter," Roger says over the phone, an hour
after I sent him a picture to confirm what I had guessed.

It circles the perimeter of a transparent cage, while
I watch it feel the smooth sides with both antennae, listening

to my friend who knows bugs as only a man whose job it is
to kill them does. "Look for sawdust along your walls,

inside your cupboards. They will chew through any wood,
but damp boards are easiest, places where rot has set in.

Have you noticed any damage around your house?" The ants,
which appear and disappear, which map the structure,

down to its last beam, the bottom-most nail, know the secrets
of my house better than I ever will. Now, the individual,

call it a scout, or lumberjack, call it a miniature Paul
Bunyan, is hanging upside down from the base

of my drinking glass, which is so thin, it looks as though
the ant has learned to walk on air, without a foothold.

It climbs down again, and pauses, facing me
like a child looking into a mirror. "You could try bait,"

Roger says, "if you don't want to spray pesticides. Powders?
It all depends on how bad the infestation is. If you do nothing,

eventually they could destroy your home." Must I
perform an exorcism, and drive you into a herd of pigs?

What do you see looking back at you? Do you recognize
your own face, or the human studying your movements—

meticulous, he can tell, desperate, determined. At what
point will you lose hope if I do not set you free? Or,

as the specialists would say, is "your hope" only my projection?
Would you just keep searching, every inch, every inch,

until you died of fatigue and hunger? "They're incredible
farmers, actually," Roger adds, off-hand. "They herd aphids

the way we do cows and sheep, and milk them, even!
It's called honeydew, the sweet liquid they take from their cattle.

Can you believe it?" My only advantage over you is size.
But smallness is to your benefit. I look closer. What seems whole

to me, and transparent, may appear to you a cloud of fractures,
thawing ice—a hairline crack is forming, you notice. Enough pressure

could widen it, enough trial and error will force a passage.
Even if you do not comprehend glass as substance,

you know that what you press against with your whole weight
is solid—you know a trap means life or death. Who says

we cannot comprehend each other's knowledge?

AFTERLIFE

> *"…We do not want to be metaphysicians."*
>   Wallace Stevens, "The Figure of the Youth as Virile Poet," Section 6

The old table, its top trying to smile
off from its base, has tiger-striped grain,
a golden sea-sand pattern, with rings
where someone set a glass of wine,
or spilled cups of Moroccan coffee,
and I wonder what Mike would think
of this piece of maple, if he saw it
shining in the October sun.
A skilled carpenter, he could refinish it.

But the table cannot hold one shape—
its legs twist and send roots under the rug.
Little hairline twigs push open the drawer.
He said wood never forgets what it was.
A board always wants to be a tree again.

CRITERIA FOR DREAMING

He dreamed of it again—the green tool box
he could not open, beneath an apple tree,
and shunned the easy symbolism of such dreams

once he woke, ashamed he could not produce,
even in sleep, an image without explanation,
one that resonated in his flesh the way a tone

can fill an instrument. He dressed. He drove
to work where all day he listened to the pulse
of pneumatic impacts, whirring like iron birds,

and dry rust broke off between his fingers,
stained almost permanently with motor oil.
His hands found tools he needed without him

looking inside the box. One after another…
As evening advanced, and rain turpentined
the streetlights, each running like a molten pin

through the dark fabric of asphalt, he saw
a cow rise up dripping from black water,
and after it a young boy ringing a bell.

FINEST CLOTHES

> *In the tradition of the Innu culture, when a man has a dream before a caribou hunt, he will tell his wife the dream, and she will interpret the images he saw, embroidering them onto her husband's hunting robe. They believe that the spirit of the Caribou sent the dream, and by wearing the robe, the hunter is paying tribute and thanks to the Caribou.*

You ask me every night in my sleep, "What will you do once you wake up?"
I have yet to answer, and keep dreaming.
So, you come to me, sometimes as my grandfather, sometimes as the woman who taught me how to read music.
You remain yourself, despite alternating faces.
Like water, you are the same through all your phases.

One night, I say enough, tell me a story instead, stop asking me what I'll do when
    morning comes.

Reclining in the darkness along my bed, you take on the appearance of my mother as she looked when I was six, and begin.
"Once there was a boy, who years later learned to interpret dreams, waiting for his father in the shade beneath a tree.
It seemed to him he was waiting all day.
Cicadas were whirring in the grass around him, above him in the branches, and this thrown voice in voiceless things made him wonder about his body and the words that filled his mouth.
Rather than undo the silence of the tree, the insects heightened it, and he realized suddenly silence is a different kind of speaking.
His father startled him.
The man approached his son with a garment in his hands.
If, at dusk, when light becomes tattered along the ground, you could pull a thread loose and unspool the sky, then you would have ready fiber to make cloth for this kind of robe.
All that color fell around the boy's shoulders."

Now, in the guise of the woman I love, you take my hand.
We stand up, and you lead me through the hallways of a quiet house.
"Careful not to wake the others sleeping," you warn.
We go outside.
It is an August afternoon.

A young man is digging in the grass, and he calls, "Be careful, there's a dry well hidden in the teasel, you'll fall in if you get too close."
But we have to walk up to the edge together, don't we?

The smell of the earth and dry grasses is like
cinnamon and caraway, iron and balsa wood.
The teasel, each tall stalk topped with a grenade
of small periwinkle flowers, grows thick.
Inextricably, we are stitched together
by a thread of fineness beyond a spider's skill to spin.
"What will you do when you wake up?"
"I will wear my thoughts as though they were my finest clothes."

ADDING SAFFRON

March brings its rain
and stubborn questions.
The red-winged blackbirds
return. I walk through
the half-thawing marsh, listening
to that familiar oak-a-lee call.
Every time the blackbird sings,
he shrugs his shoulders.
I don't know either, I tell him.
Sometimes, I think the soul
is two-toned, like an old board—
the half that's been baked by sunlight
is dark brown, the color of cinnamon,
or burnt toast, while the other half
that was covered with a stone or sheet
of plywood is light yellow, as though
the tree has just been cut—then
blackbird interrupts—
isn't this a little extravagant?
Adding "the soul" to every problem, isn't it
excessive, like including saffron threads in a dessert?
Yes, I answer, excessive—unnecessary, even
if it does impart that pretty yellow
you can't manage with other dyes,
and subtle flavor, easy to miss,
like the soul when you consider all
the ingredients for life, many
of which are strong-flavored
like garlic, or molasses…
But aren't we getting our metaphors
mixed up a little? We don't eat number two pine,
we aren't beavers, shouldn't we choose?
Is the soul a spice, or an element of architecture?
Things should be squared and orderly!
Blackbird has no response for this.
He shrugs and flashes that red stripe
as though it answers every question.
Some presence in a clump of cattails
summons him away. I ought to keep
myself focused on what's necessary,
on how to solve the problem
asked by the doctor's scalpel
when it cut my mother's womb

open and left that funny smile on her belly
that I always think of when I see
an old tree in the woods,
scarred by a line of barbed wire
its bark grew to include.
The fence is gone, but
little tines of steel show through.
I've been living ever since
with an impression—
that whatever rules
I was supposed to live
by are already
broken…But I never can
make up my mind.
I go back and forth
from an extreme of darkness
to an extreme of light.
Maybe I lack a counter-brace.
Maybe the ground isn't level.
But, I always end up adding saffron,
blaming the soul, because
it is sweet on my tongue,
and bitter in my stomach—
because it won't let me be
one thing, light or dark,
excessive, or shy.
It makes me try for both.

THE ROOFERS

Since sun-up, I've watched roofers working
at one end of my street, tipping ladders against eaves,

climbing up and down as calmly as Jacob's angels
in jeans and steel-toe boots. A surprise—

instead of the usual grades of ply,
the men uncover hardwood planks,

and now a pyramid of gold shines
in the morning light. Shingles and tar,

over one hundred degrees in the sun. Thirst
you cannot quench. Your face covered with sweat.

If you're afraid of falling, the air feels thin
and frayed, like a blue, threadbare shirt.

Your toes reflexively clench inside your boots.
The reward—your paycheck, and the vista.

I wish I had no fear of heights, like the men
I worked with for a year in Houston—Servando,

who sang mariachi while he clung to a nylon rope
thirty feet above the ground, his hammer, a metronome.

His brother Sergio one evening lay back
on a steep-pitched gable as if it were a couch

to watch the sunset. Look at that, Willie, he said,
and I managed to wedge myself into an angle

where a dormer protruded from the roof
and turned to see the Texas sky—cloudless, enormous.

I forgot where I was. Long enough to realize
I had never seen the depth and curvature of air like this.

Long enough to remember how the sky used to be
portrayed in art as a woman arching on fingertips and toes,

her body tattooed with stars. For a second, I thought
I had found Sergio's confidence—how he could lean

over the edge holding on by a nail, while chimney swifts
swooped overhead—half-convinced, he could fly too

if he reached out his arms. Then gravity reasserted itself.
I felt the heaviness of my bones—how unlike a bird's they are.

The few times I've cupped in my palms a fledgling sparrow
that had fallen from its nest, or a chickadee, I was shocked

by how light their bodies are, lighter than a tablespoon of honey.
I turned around, somehow, got down the ladder vowing

never to climb one again. From the roof, I heard
Sergio call, Oh Willie, you're missing it!

ALMOST UNMISTAKABLY

for Lech Kowalski

Wind. Flash freeze after rain.
Outdoors, trying to open a gate
latch in the dark, I wonder how
people endured the Arctic winters
with little more than whale fat,
the skin of seals, and fur
borrowed from polar bears.
The trees, when a gust picks up,
crackle with ice, but the sound
is almost unmistakably that
of fire popping in dry hardwood.
So much smoke everywhere,
it is hard to see. I make my way
through a tundra that was
my garden two months ago.
Snapped in half, dry, dark umber
stalks look like the burned spars
of a ruined village. This is not war,
it is only winter. Both come
again and again. I stand listening
to that warm, cheery hearth whisper,
then dig my way back to the house
via a different route so the wind
won't know which path to follow.

CHANGES

> *None have seen the Barnacle Goose's nest or egg; nor is this surprising since such geese are said to have spontaneous generation. When the fir masts or planks of ships have rotted in the sea, a kind of fungus breaks out upon them in which after time the form of birds may be seen; and these become clothed in feathers and eventually fly away.*
> William Turner, 16th Century English Ornithologist

They happen slowly, these changes—
so much slower than the growth of stems,
or the spiraling of a mollusk shell—
that things seem to stay the same,   nothing jars

        us toward metamorphosis,
the way, in poems, gods merely waved
careless hands and instantaneously,
a boy grew horns,
a girl felt her skin callus into bark,
or two joined together in an agony of closeness,
forming one body, born from a cold lake.

Ovid never studied taxonomy.
His hand moved with the speed of imagination,
and like all speed, it was painful, passionate.
He never went to the Galapagos,
never sat drawing bird beaks, wondering
what shapes they would take next.

Yet everything is stretching, shedding skin, breaking
out—and even we outgrow ourselves
unpredictably.

Charles, on the sloop deck, looking back to volcanic shores,
did you remember the old ornithologists
who thought geese grew from barnacles
hanging like white and gray pears on driftwood logs?
No one ever caught them in their chrysalis,
but, marvelous! — to see the shells open
and watch necks emerge like stalks
on which their bodies swell!

To observe how armor turns to down,
plumage so fine it moves in still air,
as though someone stood breathing on their bodies.

Finally, the head and beak form, with a shake, the fruit falls
and waddles toward the water where it floats,
as though to say goodbye to what it once had been.
Then, with a flashing spray,
new wings
       lift up—   fly!

BUSINESS TRIPS TO PITTSBURGH

> *"I am finally ready for the happiness I spent my youth arguing and fighting against."*
> Gerald Stern, "At Bickford's"

I sometimes think about all the shoes
I've left—lonely somewhere. Every time I go for a walk
in the marshes, I see someone's boot, or a pump
whose heel snapped in half like a dry carrot. How
do they get here, I wonder, and keep walking, because
it's the birds I came to see, not these poor ducks
minus wings, abandoned by their flocks, floating in
a little puddle. The old canal ran right through here.
It's a mucky ditch now, algae-covered
in summer. The geese seem to love it, though.
In winter, when snow covers the marsh,
you can see how straight the gouge was made, aimed
right at downtown Utica, over there in the distance.
And I like imagining the men who shoveled
all that earth when they were building the Erie—
how one of them probably sat down, sore,
and took his boots off to let his feet dry out in the sun.
He looked at some grass, some reeds, the native kind
you don't find anymore, and he noticed the little gnats
flying around his salty toes. The gnats are still here,
and so is this cricket, who doesn't realize how
out in the open it is, getting ready to start that leg thing
crickets do compulsively, the way we get chatty
on Saturday mornings…Somehow, I made my way to this
spot, which is as good a spot as any, which has as much history
as Washington, or Mosul. Granted, there was never a library
on this site, other than a library of feathers. It's getting dark.
Ducks are landing on the cold water. They probably spent
summer close to the Arctic circle, maybe on the same
rocky coast where those crazy sailors looking for
a Northwest Passage finally sat down and realized
where they were. We all do our traveling, convinced
we have a destination, but when I think about my wanderings,
I'm surprised by the mileage. Am I destined
to stay here, or am I another migrant on a layover waterway?
For some reason, many of the poets I've been reading lately
grew up in Pittsburgh—Jack Gilbert, Gerald Stern—
and James Wright lived in Martins Ferry, Ohio,
not far from that unlovingly named city. What is it

about a place that seems to produce poets? Is it the water?
Are poets water fowl, all honk and quack?
My feet aren't webbed, but I do have trouble finding
a good pair of shoes. When I told my wife about this coincidence,
she said, "Yep, you're going to leave. You'll start going on
business trips to Pittsburgh. One day, you'll forget your way home."

HOUSE BUILT ON FALLING RAIN

> *"...Es una casa / situada en los cimientos de la lluvia."*
> Pablo Neruda, "Melancolía en las Familias"

Don't look! she says,
as if she didn't know me.
I listen to her opening the closet door,
moving boxes, and watch her check over her shoulder
to see if my eyes are closed.
It's been thirty-three years since my eyes first opened—
DON'T LOOK.
Of all our commandments,
that has been the hardest for me to follow.
My curiosity is to blame, but also my admiration.
To see—to know, having seen—to worship—
these are the knots that hold this body together.

I fold my hands in my lap and wait for my wife,
peeking at her as she kneels on the floor.
She trusts me with her hiding place,
and I trust her with mine, each of us sure
the other wouldn't search for what we keep secret.

What does it mean, to watch another person?
Why is it so satisfying to see a man moving with ease,
running while looking up, reaching his hand out and catching a ball?
Why do we feel robbed when someone looks at us the wrong way?
Who hasn't watched themselves in a plate glass window
walk along a row of shops, smiling, confident, enjoying
one moment of vanity? Have we frightened ourselves
in mirrors, seen a stranger's face invading our privacy,
peering at us through our own eyes?

I look at myself, standing in the shower.
My body is slick with water, glistening like a newborn.
This human shape,
its four limbs, its curves and appendages—
how could anything so awkward and graceful have coalesced from mud?
I have said my body is held together by knots, but they are knots of water.
I live in a house built on falling rain.

It's her body I know most.
I have memorized her eyebrows.
There are moles on her cheek I love more than stars.
When she kneels like that, I can't help but look.

There are things I don't want to see.
What is the difference
between bearing witness and voyeurism?

Give me a little space, please,
the elderly patient asks her nurse,
who has already seen her body
and many like hers,
her breasts, emptied of milk years ago,
her scarred belly, her bones.
She wants to wipe herself on her own,
without help, to keep this last dignity,
not to have it taken away.
It's okay to listen, and stand nearby,
to catch her if she starts to fall
but only if you turn—draw the curtain—
shut your eyes.

Keep your eyes shut, we're told—don't look
as the powerful practice handshakes for the cameras.
Keep your eyes shut, don't look
as a man dies on the pavement beside a car.
I make myself watch.
And know what it's like
to stand beside a man, hold his hand, feel the knot of his pulse
loosen, and come undone.

It occurs to me now that her posture is one of prayer.
If I told the narrative of this evening—
a quiet celebration, dinner together, a birthday gift
it wouldn't have included this moment.
Something else is happening.
She is kneeling by the opened door of an altar.
Had I kept my eyes closed, I wouldn't have seen her like this,
unexpectedly reverent—peaceful.
And I am reminded:
it takes patience to really see.

The stories I remember most are about vision:
the hunter profanes a goddess with his eyes
and becomes the hunted,
a buck, torn apart by his own dogs.
A woman turns to watch a city burn, and hardens into salt.

But stories imply
a witness. One at least
who survives, changed
not by a miracle, but by sight.
Having seen the column of salt, he has seen the destruction of the city.
Every deer carcass is the untied body of a young man.
Its eyes are human eyes,
and they are always open.

At last, finding what she kept hidden,
my wife stands and I squeeze my eyelids shut.
You peeked, didn't you?
I deny her accusation—
of course not, you know me, I like surprises!
Crossing the room, she stands in front of me.
I can feel her there, holding out her hands.
As she places the gift in mine,
her fingertips touch my palms.
She asks, are you ready?

i From the film *Andrei Tarkovsky: A Cinema Prayer,* (2019)
ii H.D. "The Walls Do Not Fall" 4.43-46
iii Edwin G. Burrows, *Forgotten Patriots: The Untold Story of American Prisoners During the Revolutionary War.*
iv The unofficial title of a painting by Cy Twombly housed at the Menil Collection, Houston, TX.
v Hohner Harmonicas are a prime example of German quality work.
vi paraphrase from an article in *The New York Times*, "Biden Warns Russia Against Using Nuclear Weapons," October 25, 2022
vii paraphrase from an article in *The Guardian* "Russia Steps Up Ukraine "Dirty Bomb" Claim in Letter to U.N." October 25, 2022
viii Emily Dickinson, poem #319
ix Lech Kowalski, from an email dated August 9, 2022
x The lines in quotes are borrowed from *The Epic of Gilgamesh* (trans. Maureen Gallery Kovacs) lines 85-86; "Song of Myself," 1855 version, by Walt Whitman, line 468; and The Book of Judges (KJV) 16:17.
xi Information regarding the word "xoc" and its possible influence on English "shark" is drawn from *Breaking the Maya Code* by Michael D. Coe, p. 141.
xii From "The Song of Wandering Aengus," by W.B. Yeats.
xiii Dead Horse Bay is a small body of water on the southern end of Brooklyn, NY. It was the site of a 19th century rendering plant, and 20th century landfill. The beach is littered with garbage, mostly broken glass and ceramic.
xiv A Russian word without parallel in English. It is often roughly translated as melancholy, sadness, listlessness, or other such, but these do not convey its full meaning, which encompasses a spiritual dimension these words lack.
xv Robert Bly, "The Difficult Word"

ACKNOWLEDGMENTS:

Thank you to the editors of the following journals in which some of these poems first appeared, often in earlier versions.

Adelaide Literary Award Anthology, 2020:	"The Border"
Belle Ombre:	"Changes"
Blue Moon Literary and Art Review:	"Starch Factory Creek"
The Bookends Review:	"Adding Saffron"
Burningword Literary Journal:	"The Pearl of Great Price"
Cider Press Review:	"Poem to the Mouse in My Attic"
The Comstock Review:	"New York Route 29, North of Fairfield"
The Decadent Review:	"Icons"
Hole in the Head Review:	"San Felipe," "A Found Photo, Dated 1919, Holland Patent, NY," and "Higby Road at Night
Little Patuxent Review:	"Steadfast Honey"
Nine Mile Magazine:	"What Endures," "Inheritance," "Nineteen Orchard Street," "One of Those Guys," "Dead Horse Bay," "Horses," "Familiar Lightning"
Offcourse:	"Egg Timer," "Ikebana," "Criteria for Dreaming," "In Praise"
Rust & Moth:	"Andrei," "Xoc/Shark"
Sangam Literary Magazine:	"The New Tenants"
Stone Canoe:	"The Exile," "Hohner Owner," "House Built on Falling Rain," "Cain"
the Thieving Magpie:	"Anamnesis"

Thimble Literary Magazine: "Freida," (under the title "The Lares"), "Vox, Vocis"

Willawaw Journal: "Say Goodbye, Catullus, to the Shores of Asia Minor"

Willows Wept Review: "Earth Science," "The Appearance of Plenty"

William Welch lives in Utica, NY where he works as a registered nurse. His poetry has appeared in various journals, including *Little Patuxent Review, Stone Canoe, Rust & Moth*, and *Cider Press Review. Adding Saffron* (Finishing Line Press, 2025) is his first full length collection. He is poetry editor for *Doubly Mad* (doublymad.org). Find more about him on his website, williamfwelch.com.

www.ingramcontent.com/pod-product-compliance
Lightning Source LLC
Chambersburg PA
CBHW020337170426
43200CB00006B/416